THE RIGHT CAREER FOR ME

I0801735

HAIRSTYLIST

KATHLEEN A. KLATTE

ROSEN PUBLISHING

Published in 2024 by The Rosen Publishing Group, Inc.
2544 Clinton Street, Buffalo, NY 14224

Copyright © 2024 by The Rosen Publishing Group, Inc.

Portions of this work were originally authored by Bridget Heos and published as *A Career as a Hairstylist*. All new material in this edition was authored by Kathleen A. Klatte.

Cover Designer: Michael Flynn
Intertior Designer: Rachel Rising
Editor: Kathleen A. Klatte

All rights reserved. No part of this book may be reproduced in any form without permission in writing from the publisher, except by a reviewer.

Cataloging-in-Publication Data

Names: Klatte, Kathleen A.
Title: Hairstylist / Kathleen A. Klatte.
Description: New York : Rosen Publishing, 2024. | Series: The right career for me | Includes glossary and index.
Identifiers: ISBN 9781499475814 (pbk.) | ISBN 9781499475821 (library bound) | ISBN 9781499475838 (ebook)
Subjects: LCSH: Hairdressing--Vocational guidance--Juvenile literature. | Barbering--Vocational guidance--Juvenile literature. | Beauty operators--Juvenile literature. | Barbers--Juvenile literature.
Classification: LCC TT958.K53 2024 | DDC 646.7'24--dc23

Some of the images in this book illustrate individuals who are models. The depictions do not imply actual situations or events.

Manufactured in the United States of America

CPSIA Compliance Information: Batch #CWRYA24. For further information, contact Rosen Publishing at 1-800-237-9932.

Find us on

CONTENTS

INTRODUCTION

Are you the one your friends come to for advice about hair and makeup? Are you up on the latest fashions and clever with your hands? Do you like working with people—helping them look great and feel great about themselves? If so, then a career as a hairstylist or barber might be right for you.

A salon or barber shop is a vital part of the community. For elderly people, getting their hair cut or styled might be one of their major social interactions. Busy professionals or parents value the chance to relax and have someone take care of them. And people of all ages rely on their hairstylist to make them look great for their special occasions.

Licensed beauticians and cosmetologists can work as hairstylists, barbers, aestheticians (doing facials), makeup artists, and nail technicians. Although beauticians and cosmetologists might be required to pass the same licensing exam, beauty professionals recognize a difference. Beauticians are trained to care for hair and skin. Cosmetologists receive more extensive training that includes makeup and nail treatments, in addition to hair and skin care.

This book focuses on careers in hairstyling and barbering. Hairstylists cut, color, and style hair, and do chemical treatments such as straightening and permanents. Barbers specialize in haircuts and shaves.

People like to look their best—whether it's for a special occasion or just their day-to-day life.

Financially speaking, hairstyling is a sound career choice. People will always want their hair done. You might recall news stories from the recent COVID-19 pandemic. Many people were upset that salons and barber shops needed to close due to public health concerns. Most people are unable to give themselves stylish haircuts, so they turn to a professional. If that pro is friendly and does a great job, then they'll stick with them for years.

Aside from economic stability, a hairstyling career allows people to provide an important service. There is a saying that "beauty is only skin deep," but the fact is, people feel better when they look good. That's why nursing homes often have a beautician who visits regularly to give shampoos and haircuts. It's also why cancer hospitals have beauty programs for their patents.

People usually think of beauticians as working in a salon, but there are other career options as well. These include selling cosmetic products or being a stylist for magazines, television, or movies. Some work in spas, hotels, resorts, or even on cruise ships.

Whatever career path hairstylists choose, working well with people is essential. Just as no two heads of hair are alike, no two people are, either. Some clients—especially the elderly who don't get out much—might want to talk. Others want some peace and quiet to read a book during their appointment. Some bring a picture of the exact hairstyle they want, while others are vague. Most of the time, hairstylists need to balance what the clients want with knowledge of what will look great on them. This is where it helps to be comfortable chatting with customers—you may know a style will look fabulous on your client, but does it suit her lifestyle? For instance, a busy mother of young children might want a style that's strictly "wash and go."

Those who work in a salon or barbershop share close quarters with other stylists, who also have different personalities and senses of style. Getting to know clients and coworkers—and their unique hairstyle needs—is part of the fun!

Today's barbers are called upon to create men's styles every bit as trendy as the ladies.

A HISTORY OF HAIRSTYLES

Hairstyles have been part of human culture for thousands of years. Artwork depicts ancient Egyptians wearing straight or braided hairstyles with bangs. They also wore wigs made of human or animal hair dyed black.

The ancient Greeks and Romans wore their hair in elaborate buns and updos trimmed with ribbons, flowers, or jewels. The Greeks used herbs, oils, and scented water to treat their hair. The Romans used curling tongs on their hair. They also wore makeup.

Surviving artwork and literature from the Heian Period (794–1192) in Japan contains records of a preference for very long straight hair—sometimes floor length! This look was achieved by combing the hair several times a day to spread natural oils from the scalp.

Contrary to what Hollywood might have you believe, medieval women didn't wear their hair long and loose. Neither was it filthy. Medieval women used combs and herbal mixtures to clean and care for their hair. They generally wore their hair braided and covered with a wimple, veil, or headdress, depending on the woman's social status. Although there are portraits, usually Italian, that show young women with long, loose hair dressed with pearls or jewels, it's thought that these are wedding portraits, not daily fashions.

French queen Marie Antoinette's personal hairdresser, Léonard Autié, created many of her iconic styles.

In African cultures, healthy, beautiful hair was treasured. Animal fat, butter, and a natural hair product called chebe powder were used to treat hair. Braiding and elaborate hairstyles were used to denote rank and marital status. Sadly, many of these traditions were lost due to the activities of European enslavers.

During the Edo Period (1603–1867) in Japan, ladies began to treat their hair with camellia oil. They also started wearing their hair pinned or tied up in elaborate styles.

Kings and queens set the fashions in Europe, and from the Renaissance on, that included wigs. The elaborate, jeweled hairstyles in many portraits of Queen Elizabeth I (1533–1603) of England are generally thought to have been wigs. The Sun King Louis XIV (1638–1715) of France wore his hair in long, dark curls—and had wigs made in the style when his own hair receded.

The 18th century is famous for elaborate ladies' hairstyles, often built up over a wire frame. Often, these were wigs. Men also wore curled and powdered wigs. These hairstyles, and the ornate clothing that accompanied them were swept away in the aftermath of the French Revolution.

The next big fashion wave from Europe was called Regency, Empire, or Federal depending on where you lived. It featured loose, high-waisted gowns and hair swept up into soft buns, reminiscent of designs seen in ancient Roman statuary.

This fashion lasted about 20 years, then styles began to develop into the Victorian look of full skirts and bonnets that's preserved in early photographs.

CHAPTER ONE

CHOOSING THE RIGHT SCHOOL

Attending a cosmetology school takes about a year and is likely to cost between $5,000-$15,000. The cost depends on the location of the school and if it's part of a university or trade school. Schools attached to famous cosmetic brands such as Aveda or Sassoon might cost upwards of $20,000. Students can pay for accredited beauty programs with loans or Pell Grants.

Even if you've been doing your friends' hair for years, cosmetology school starts from the basics. You'll learn to do things in a way that's safe and sanitary—not just stylish.

Although cosmetology school costs considerably less than a four-year college degree, it's a lot of money, and you want to think carefully before you make a commitment. This quiz will help you decide.

What is your view of beauty?

A. When you look your best, you are beautiful.
B. Either you're born with it or you're not.
C. Beauty is on the inside. It doesn't matter how you look on the outside.

For how many hours a day would you be willing or able to be on your feet?

A. Up to twelve.
B. Four.
C. Eight.

Which schedule would you be happy with?

A. Working the hours that are convenient for your customers.
B. Nine to five, Monday through Friday.
C. Making your own hours.

How would you prefer to spend your day?

A. Talking to others.
B. Working quietly and independently.
C. Half and half.

If you answered A to all these questions, then this career might be a good fit. You can also talk to your hairstylist or barber about their careers and ask if you can observe them one day. Once you're sure about your decision, it's time to start looking at schools.

Schools in places such as Los Angeles or Manhattan may cost more than other locations. Room and board are also likely to be expensive.

Once you're sure you want to pursue a career as a hairstylist, you need to consider your options—and your budget. Is there a trade or vocational high school in your area with a cosmetology program? What are the enrollment requirements? Wil you be prepared to take your state license after graduation, or will you need to take more classes elsewhere? High school programs can be judged in the same way post-secondary programs are. If it meets your needs, it would be a good deal financially. High school programs are not only free, but they also allow cosmetologists to earn money a year earlier.

Some school districts and high schools may not offer cosmetology programs. That's OK—there's plenty in the standard high school curriculum to prepare you for beauty school. Art classes are an obvious choice. Math and business classes are useful, too. Depending on your employment status, you may be responsible for billing customers, marketing your services, or ordering supplies. And don't discount everyone's favorite—physical education (PE). Being a barber or hairstylist means spending a lot of time on your feet!

Some beauty schools allow students to enroll at 16 years of age. Others require a high school diploma or General Educational Development (GED). Use the internet to see what schools are available in your area, how much they cost, and if they allow dual enrollment—that is, attendance while you're still in high school.

Not all your clients will be fashion-conscious adults. You'll also learn to work with squirming kids.

State boards license cosmetologists and barbers, and schools are geared toward the requirements of their respective states. Students planning to attend school and work in different states should find out if they'll need additional credits. If you're dreaming of a career in film or theatre, check out the International Alliance of Stage Employees, Moving Picture Technicians, Artists and Allied Crafts of the United States and Canada (IATSE). This is the trade union that represents hair and makeup artists in the entertainment industry.

If you're planning to attend school in a different state than where you live, remember that room and board will be a significant expense. To find a cosmetology or barber school in any state, go to the website of the state's cosmetology or barber board. (Sometimes they are the same.) When seeking schools elsewhere, check the websites of the National Cosmetology Association, the Beauty Schools Directory (which includes beauty and barber colleges), or area community colleges. Community colleges cost more for non-resident students.

Once you have a list of possible schools, you'll want to consider several factors. First, will you attend barber school or cosmetology school? Both teach how to cut, color, perm, and style men's and women's hair. Barber colleges also teach shaving and business courses related to running a barbershop. In some cases, barbers learn skin and nail care. If you have a definite career goal, think about what will help the most. Do you want a steady job in your community? Your own business? Or do you have more adventurous plans? Cosmetology programs also teach manicuring, facials, makeup art, and waxing. Those interested in business courses related to owning or managing a salon might want to enroll in an entrepreneurial program at a community college.

In beauty school, you'll start out learning hair cutting and styling techniques using mannequins.

Next, you'll want to look at the program. How much hands-on training will you get? How often will you work on mannequins? Other students' hair? Walk-in customers? Is the lab up to date? How does the school teach customer service, people skills, business skills, and marketing? How does the school prepare students for the licensing exam? What is the passing rate? Does the school offer interview preparation and career counseling? What is the job placement rate? What is the student-teacher ratio? Who are the teachers? It's a good idea to visit the school to see if it's the right fit. Is it clean and organized? Do the students seem happy?

You should also consider practical matters. If you don't have a car, can you take public transportation to the school? How much does the school cost? (When attending a junior college, in-state tuition is cheaper.) How much will your textbooks cost? What supplies will you need to provide? Students can seek the same financial aid through the U.S. Department of Education for cosmetology school as they would for a four-year college. Many beauty schools and beauty organizations offer scholarships specifically for cosmetology. At community colleges, general scholarships may also apply. Some schools also offer part-time programs, which allow students to work while attending school.

Check school websites for information on how and when to enroll and how to seek financial aid. Your guidance counselor should be able to help you gather some of this information. Once admitted, you're in for a fun—but challenging—experience.

Aside from all the artistic skills, you'll also learn how to clean and sanitize your tools and workstation.

WHAT HAPPENS IN CLASS?

You should allow a full year to complete a cosmetology or barber program if you plan to attend full time. The exact length of the program will vary somewhat, depending on the licensing requirements of the state where the school is located. A program offered by a community college or continuing education program might cover only the licensing requirements. A dedicated cosmetology school, especially one associated with a major salon brand, might cover more topics.

The total credit hours needed vary by state. Usually, it's between 1,000 and 1,600 hours. A barbering program might require fewer hours. Hours are divided into three areas: theory (learned in a classroom), lab (which involves working on mannequins or other students), and clinical (which involves working on customers). Cosmetology schools usually have their own shop or salon.

Cosmetology school is hands-on. Far from being stuck in a classroom, students spend most of their time in the lab or clinic. Right away, they work on mannequins, soon after, on other students, and, finally, on customers.

Students learn how to cut, color, style, perm, and relax all different hair types. Working with natural or ethnic hair is becoming part of the standard curriculum in beauty schools, rather than a specialty. Students also learn how to practice safety and sanitation. This has always been an important part of working in a salon or barber shop, but since the COVID-19 pandemic, sanitizing tools, chairs, and surfaces between clients has become imperative.

They also study people skills. For instance, in schools that use certain textbooks, they learn that there are four basic personality types: the executive, the caretaker, the fun-loving person, and the worker. They learn how to relate to each. For example, the fun-loving client craves friendly conversation, while the executive focuses on the task at hand. Your future clients might range from grandparents eager to chatter about their grandkids, teens who want the same look as their favorite actor or rock star, and youngsters who'd rather be anywhere but your chair.

To some degree, cosmetology students learn business skills, too. This includes things such as accounting and taxes. Marketing—both traditional and online—is indispensable. Developing your brand and creating a portfolio are also skills you'll need.

Finally, they practice the grunt work that hairstyling entails, such as sweeping the floor, washing towels, and keeping their booth stocked and clean. (Seriously—get used to washing towels. You'll be doing that regardless of whether you're styling hair in a salon or a theater!)

Cleaning up is a huge part of cosmetology. Think about it—would you want your hair done someplace with clippings all over the floor or things dripped on the counter?

LEO PASSAGE AND PIVOT POINT

Pivot Point is one of the major names in beauty education. Belgian hairdresser Leo Passage (1936–2011) founded the school in 1962. Passage won more than 100 European hairdressing competitions. The magazine *Modern Salon* named him one of the top 50 hairdressers of all time.

Passage wrote about his methods in a book called *The Scientific Approach to Hair Design*. This approach began to be taught in other beauty schools in the late 1960s. In the 1970s, Pivot Point began manufacturing mannequins for use by beauty school students. They also turned their attention to becoming environmentally friendly.

Today Pivot Point continues to make its mark not only as a leader in beauty education, but also in its dedication to the use of sustainable supplies and ethically sourced labor.

For textbooks, schools usually use ones published by Milady or Pivot Point. Let's look briefly at *Milady's Standard Cosmetology*. The 14th edition, published in 2022, is two volumes and is also available digitally. The *Cosmetology* volume starts out with the history of cosmetology. The next section is "Health Sciences," focusing on skin, hair, and nails. Students learn how nutrition affects hair, skin, and nails.

Students start out practicing on mannequins. Soon they'll style their classmates' hair, then eventually customers.

The next section focuses on "Hair Services." This includes shampooing, principles of design (such as which cuts work best with which facial features), and how to do different haircuts, styles, and treatments—such as the long layered cut, the French twist, and chemical relaxer treatments. It also teaches how to color hair and cut and fit wigs.

The last two sections of the *Cosmetology* book are "Skin Care Services" and "Nail Services." The *Foundations* volume covers business and practical concerns such as professional image and communications. It also covers infection control, and chemical and electrical safety. It concludes with career planning and business information.

In the lab, students practice hairstyling techniques. Using other students as models, students experiment with different styles and colors. One of the goals of training is to learn to handle all types of hair.

Often, students attend cosmetology school with the same small group of students. They might become good friends—but they might also have personality conflicts. From this experience, students learn to see things from different points of view and to accept people as they are. What matters is that everyone does their job in a safe, professional manner.

In the hair clinic, students serve customers with a variety of hair needs. This is their chance to practice listening. The customer might say, "I want a short, layered haircut" or "I just want a no-fuss style." Either of those statements can mean lots of things. The student-stylists need to draw out more details or make suggestions. The customer might ask for a hairstyle made popular by a movie star. If that look isn't right for the customer's facial features or hair type, the student needs to say so tactfully.

BEYOND THE CLASSROOM

It's important to make the most of cosmetology school. Arrive on time and stay on top of the details that make the day go smoothly, such as keeping a supply of fresh towels. Get to know professors, classmates, and clients. Hairstyling is a very people-focused career—your instructors will have valuable insights on dealing with customers. You'll eventually encounter cranky and difficult people, so don't be afraid to ask someone with experience for advice.

Join a professional organization, such as the Professional Beauty Association, the American Barber Association, or the United Professional

A LOOK INSIDE COSMETOLOGY SCHOOL

Cosmetology school is an investment of time and money—an investment in your future. You want to be sure you get the most out of your experience. Even though it's shorter and less expensive than a four-year college, you still need to work to be successful.

Here are some words of wisdom from a beauty school instructor:

"It [cosmetology] should be something you're drawn to. You should be visual and creative and have a hands-on learning style. You don't have to be good at cutting hair right away. Some students pick it up quickly; others work and work and work. By the time they finish school, you can't tell the difference. Their work has the same quality."

And some advice from a student.

"You have to be a team player. If your classmates are running behind, help them, and they'll do the same for you. Being optimistic is a huge thing. If you doubt yourself, you'll never make it. Be open-minded. There are so many ways to do things, and there is so much more to learn than you think there is going to be.

"No matter how frustrated you get, it is critical to practice, practice, practice. You cannot practice enough. It's not only how well you do it but also how quickly you can do it.

"Know that you'll have to work hard and maybe a lot of hours—possibly evenings and weekends—and be excited about it. If you're bummed out, it will show. Be willing to pay your dues and be excited to help your customers and coworkers."

Today, barbers and hairstylists are taught to style and care for every type of hair.

Barbers and Cosmetologists Association. Learn to take before and after photos of clinic work so you can create a portfolio to show employers. Visit salons to learn how they operate. Have a career goal in mind, and know the steps needed to get there. Begin researching job opportunities while you're still in school. Meet with a representative in your school placement office regularly. Arrange for an internship. Keep in mind that finding a good job is a full-time job.

Toward the end of cosmetology or barber school, students take a written and possibly a practical exam administered by their state board. The written exam is based on textbook material. Milady and Pivot Point as well as other companies publish cosmetology exam prep books. Questions cover topics such as professional image, sanitation, properties of the hair and scalp, draping, shampooing, cutting, artistry in hairstyling, wet hairstyling, heat hairstyling, permanents, relaxing, straightening, coloring, and artificial hair.

In New York state, applicants are required to be at least 17 years old, have completed a 1,000-hour training program, and passed a health exam. The written exam is multiple choice and takes 2.5 hours. For the practical exam, instructors expect students to bring their own supplies and dress appropriately for salon work. They're judged on how well they perform a list of cosmetology tasks, but also on their appearance, how well they set up and clean up their work area, and adherence to health and safety protocols throughout the exam.

Graduating is only the beginning. Styles change quickly and hairstylists must be familiar with all the latest looks—and how to execute them. Dealing with people in this age of instant, online reviews is also an ongoing process. Once you start your first job, you may find that a particular facet of cosmetology interests you enough to take additional special classes.

Even in your neighborhood beauty parlor, you'll need to be on top of all the latest digital trends. People expect to connect to your website and social media.

CHAPTER TWO

STARTING YOUR CAREER

Choosing to do something you love as a career is a good move. You want to be excited to get up and go to work every morning—after all, you're going to be doing it for a long time. However, what separates a career from a hobby is being paid a living wage for your efforts.

The Bureau of Labor Statistics is part of the U.S. Department of Labor. It's an official government agency and its website is a solid source of information for the range of salary you can expect as a hairstylist and projections for new job openings. But numbers on a page can only tell you so much. To get an idea of how easy it will be to get a job, take a good look around your community.

If you live in a large municipality, there are probably multiple chain salons, a spa or two, and maybe department stores or hotels with their own salons. But what if you live in a small town? What if most ladies have been going to the beauty parlor on Main Street for years? You might have to work a bit harder for your chance, but you can still have the career you want.

Talk to people. For starters, talk to the local beautician. She might be looking for someone new to attract younger or different clientele. Or perhaps there's an underserved segment of the community. Talk to your friends. Do some of them have to travel to a different community to find a beautician who provides the services they want?

THINKING OUTSIDE THE BOX

Kinky Boots is a 2005 movie and 2012 Broadway musical based on actual events. A man inherits his family's shoe factory only to learn that no one is interested in buying the kind of shoes they make. So, he does some investigating, finds a new niche audience, and his factory starts making boots for drag queens.

Even if you live in a small community, there's room for you. You just need to find your own niche audience. Perhaps it's working with natural or ethnic hair. Are you good with kids? Maybe it's a shop that specializes in children's haircuts and has a play area for kids while their parents are getting their hair done. Or maybe it's not a shop at all. Maybe your town could use a hairdresser who visits those who don't leave home. Or one who does hair and makeup for wedding parties? Keep an open mind and you'll find your opportunity—or make it!

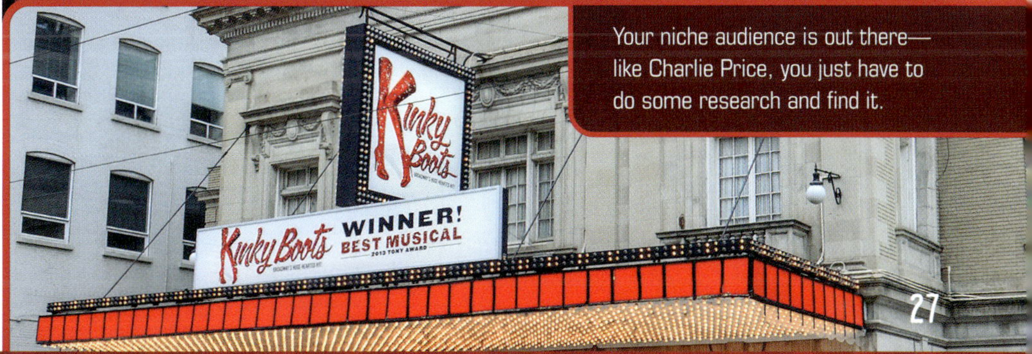

Your niche audience is out there—like Charlie Price, you just have to do some research and find it.

Ask your friends—and maybe even your parent's friends. If people need to go to a different town to get their ethnic or natural hair styled that could be the perfect niche audience for your talents.

You know you want a career in beauty—that's a great place to start. But where do you picture yourself five or ten years down the road? Would you like to run your own shop or spa? Or leave the business end of things to someone else and concentrate on styling hair? Do you want to focus all your energy on your career? Or do you want a solid job where you can set your own hours while leaving time for a family? There are no wrong answers. You just need to think about what's right for you.

Whatever your dream is, write it down. Next, think about what steps will take you there. For example, if in five years you would like to work in an upscale salon, a first step would be to seek an internship or assistant position in one. If no such positions are available, you could still ask the manager for an informational interview. This is not a job interview. Instead, it's a chance to express your interest in the salon and find out what experience you would need to work there. The manager might suggest that you take additional classes or that you have a certain amount of professional experience before they consider hiring you. This is all good information that will help you on your career path.

Next, think about what you want from your first job. Are there a range of shops and salons in your area? Or are you looking for something special, like working in the theater? Are you willing to relocate? How far are you willing to commute? What realistic salary range are you seeking? Which benefits are essential to you? What atmosphere are you looking for?

If you enjoy the excitement of weddings and proms, you might choose a salon that specializes in doing hair for these events. If you prefer a more laid-back atmosphere, a neighborhood salon might be best. If possible, visit the salon before you apply. Ask yourself if you would like to be a client here. Do the employees seem happy? Is it a friendly atmosphere? Are there red flags, such as bad sanitation, rude employees, or an apparent lack of business? Your first job might not be your dream job, but it should be one that you can enjoy and learn from.

WEDDING STYLES

Are you at your best when working under pressure? Are you in love with the idea of making people look wonderful for the most important day of their life? Maybe being a wedding stylist is the right choice for you. Brides today often choose to have a stylist or team of stylists come to their home or hotel to do their hair and makeup for their wedding. Services may be booked just for the bride, or for the entire wedding party.

This career path requires a good head for management and contracts (or a good business manager to handle that end of things for you), diplomacy (to deal with people on a very emotional day), and an ability to roll with whatever craziness comes your way.

A wedding stylist doesn't just make the bride look amazing—they make sure her look will hold up through what is often a very long day.

THE JOB HUNT

Today, most people start their job hunt online. LinkedIn is a social media platform designed for business connections. You can create a résumé, set alerts for job listings, and follow big beauty brands. Indeed is another site where you can search job listings by industry and location. Many cosmetology and barber organizations and websites also post jobs.

You can also find jobs by networking, whether online or in person. For instance, a salon owner might post a help wanted notice in their shop or on one of their social media platforms. Keeping in touch with classmates and teachers may also provide job leads.

A common first job for hairstylists is to work at a national chain or as an assistant at a salon. Spas, department stores, hotels, and even cruise ships may have entry-level positions open, too.

To apply for a job, you should write a professional-looking résumé. It should include information about your education, work, and volunteer experience. This can seem difficult at first, but there are books and online tutorials available. Word processing programs have templates you can adapt. Your school might have someone who can help with the process, or you can check your local library to see if they have a program.

You'll also need a cover letter. This should explain why all of your experience and education make you a good candidate for the job. The letter should be tailored to fit each job you apply for. You should also have a list of references—teachers or supervisors who have agreed to give you a positive recommendation.

You don't necessarily need to wear a suit to interview at a salon, but your clothes should be neat, and your hair, makeup, and nails should be stylish.

THE INTERVIEW

Applying for your first job is both exciting and nerve wracking. While you're waiting to hear back about job applications, be mindful of how you answer your phone or perhaps set up a basic polite voicemail message. If responding via email, be sure to reread your response and check the spelling before hitting send. Or consider setting up a separate account for use on job applications. (Your name) @ (Free Email Service) works fine. Something that's too cutesy or uses rude words can make a bad impression on prospective employers.

Any job interview involves lots of questions. Some are common to any interview: Tell me about yourself. Why do you want to work here? Others are more particular to the job in question: What are your strengths as a hairstylist? What did you like about cosmetology school? What didn't you like? These questions should be answered honestly and positively. Never speak badly of anyone in an interview. A positive answer to "What didn't you like about cosmetology school?" might be: "I'd been styling my friends and family's hair throughout high school. Relearning how to do that was hard at first, but I was excited to learn the right techniques." This shows that the job seeker saw the challenge as an opportunity.

Since interviewees are in the beauty business, they should look and act the part. Don't chew gum and allow yourself plenty of time to get to the interview. A stylish haircut and manicured nails are important. Courtesy and self-confidence should be shown to everyone. The interview starts in the parking lot. The manager or the salon's best customer might be pulling in at the same time. Trying to beat someone to the last parking space or letting the door swing in someone's face won't make a good first impression!

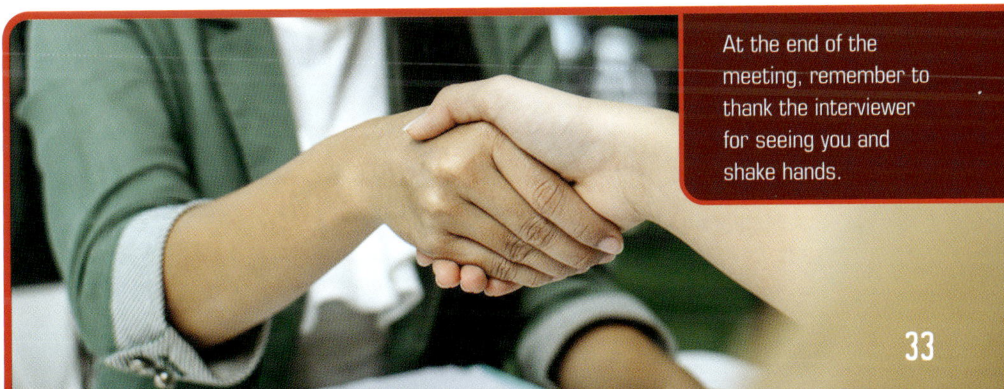

At the end of the meeting, remember to thank the interviewer for seeing you and shake hands.

VIDAL SASSOON AND HIS GEOMETRIC HAIRCUTS

Vidal Sassoon (1928–2012) is one of the great innovators of the modern salon styling industry. He pioneered what came to be known as "precision cutting"—designing a haircut based on the client's bone structure. He designed his cuts to be "wash and wear" to suit the needs of modern career women.

Hairstyles of the 1950s involved curlers, teasing, and lots of hairspray—plus frequent trips to the beauty parlor. Sassoon's 1960s bobs and pixie cuts did away with all that, although the short styles required trims every six weeks or so, keeping his stylists in business.

In the 1980s, Sassoon became a household name in beauty. Sassoon styling products were advertised on television and sold in supermarkets. The Sassoon name even appeared on a line of jeans!

Vidal Sassoon was one of the first stylists to become a celebrity in his own right.

Consumers in the mid-1980s were very familiar with Sassoon's slogan "If you don't look good, we don't look good." Sassoon products are still sold worldwide.

The interviewer will probably ask job seekers if they have any questions. Asking something shows interest and helps the job seekers decide whether the salon is right for them. (Job seekers are interviewing the salon, too!) You might ask if the salon promotes from within—in other words, could you become part of the management team someday? Or if the salon will pay for you to take additional classes, or how soon you might get to work on a special event, such as a wedding party.

HOW WILL YOU BE PAID?

Job applicants should wait until they are offered a job to ask about salary. However, if the employer didn't provide the information in the ad for the position, they can ask basic questions, such as, "Are your employees paid salaries, commission, or both?" Salons and barbershops handle employee compensation in a variety of ways, including:

- **Salary or hourly wage only.** Employees receive a steady paycheck no matter how many clients they have. Tips, of course, vary according to their number of customers. Taxes are calculated and withheld by the employer and you are issued a paycheck via paper check or direct deport.

- **Salary plus commission.** Employees get paid a base salary or wage plus a percentage of the amount each customer pays.

- **Salary for hairstyling plus commission on hair products sold.** This is the same as the salary or hourly wage-only model. However, employees also earn a percentage of the dollar amount of hair products they sell. This encourages employees to recommend products to their clients.

- **Commission only.** Employees may take home 30 to 50 percent of whatever clients pay. If there are no clients, employees don't get paid.

- **Independent contractor.** A salon might hire independent contractors for busy times, such as prom season or wedding season. Independent contractors work for themselves. They're paid the amount agreed upon in their contract and handle their own taxes.

- **Booth rental.** Workers rent their space and keep whatever clients pay. Income is 100 percent determined by the number of clients. Workers pay their own taxes and purchase their own equipment. They are not employees.

Typically, first-year workers should not rent a booth or work on commission only. Without an established clientele, it's too risky.

Ways to find hairstyling and barber jobs include networking and searching online job boards and classifieds. Networking helps to develop important contacts for the future.

DECIDING WHERE TO APPLY

When you're trying to decide where to apply for a job, online reviews on sites such as Yelp or Google can be very helpful. Not every review will be positive—that's normal. Sometimes people just aren't happy with the way their hair turned out. There will be reviews posted by people who were angry that the salon was closed during a major storm, or that they wouldn't accept a walk-in five minutes before closing.

You want to read enough reviews, good and bad, to make sure there isn't a pattern of complaints about rude employees or the shop being dirty.

After the interview, send a thank-you note. An email is fine. Thank the interviewer for their time and let them know you look forward to hearing from them. There are books and websites you can refer to for interview etiquette.

Once you're offered the job, you'll be quoted a salary, hourly wage, or commission rate. If this is your first job, your pay will be on the lower end of the scale. Check the BLS website to have an idea of what's appropriate.

If you're offered a written contract, take the time to read and understand it. Don't be afraid to ask your parents to go over it with you. You'll want to understand things such as how long you'll be "on probation." (With many companies, it's 90 days.)

Will you be paid for holidays? Which ones? Will you have any benefits, such as health insurance? Will you get an employee discount?

Is the salon clean and neat? Are the employees friendly and well-groomed? Does it seem like a place you'd like to spend 40 hours a week?

CHAPTER THREE

YOU GOT THE JOB!

Starting a new job is a grand adventure. You get to use your new skills and you get paid. When people ask what you do, you can introduce yourself as a professional hairstylist. All of that feels pretty good. Of course, since you're the new person, you're at the bottom of the barber pole, so to speak. Often staff members with the most seniority get the first pick of what hours they work and what days off they want.

You may find yourself working weird hours or taking drop-in clients—and that's good. It gives you a range of experience, and a chance to find your niche. A mother might bring her two-year-old child for his first haircut. If you're an experienced babysitter or older sibling, you can put those skills to good use. Or maybe you get an elderly woman whose only outings are to the doctor, church, and the beauty parlor. She's excited to chat with you and peruse the new magazines in the waiting area. She wants a hairstyle that's not your specialty, but you'll give it your best shot. A teenager might drop in. She needs a prom updo, and she forgot to make an appointment. She's panicking.

These clients will each teach you something—whether it's about hair or people. These "one-time" visitors might also become lifelong clients. For instance, the girl getting a prom updo might usually have her mom color her hair. But if the hairstylist helps the girl with her prom emergency, she'll return for her next color job. Or maybe the mom of the young boy had been to two other places, and no one could get her child to sit still long enough for the haircut. As drop-in customers begin requesting you, you will build a clientele.

A new hairstylist or barber's schedule will likely include evenings or weekends. Days before holidays, such as the days before Thanksgiving and Christmas Eve, will be busy because people take off work and want to look nice for get-togethers. If a hairstylist does prom or wedding updos, Fridays and Saturdays will be busy, especially during spring.

Maybe that annoying early morning shift that no one else wants is perfect for a client who works overnights. You know what they say about life handing you lemons—make yourself some lemonade. Or in this case, build your own client base.

Even though you've graduated, you've still got a lot of learning to do. Fashions change quickly and you need to stay up to date on hairstyling trends. You should follow fashion magazines and watch red carpet events to see what the stars look like. You should also attend conferences and trade shows. At these shows, you can see the latest styles and products demonstrated. To practice these, stylists can ask their salon manager if they can have a model night, where people volunteer to let cosmetologists try new styles on them. Workers should take advantage of any training sessions offered in the salon. They should learn techniques that help them work faster, allowing them to see more clients.

Much of what you'll learn your first year doesn't have to do with hair. It's about people and communication. You'll learn how to make your clients feel comfortable by being friendly and positive. You'll learn to find out what clients want by asking if they prefer a big change or a trim, for instance. And you'll learn how to tactfully tell a client that the high maintenance, product-laden hairdo that movie star just got might not be right for them, as well as how to encourage them to try something that works with their looks and lifestyle.

Sometimes, there might be miscommunication between a stylist and a client who doesn't like their haircut. The client might be angry. The stylist should keep their cool and offer to make adjustments. They can state their case calmly but shouldn't argue with the client. If the client wants to talk to a manager, they should be allowed to talk without interruption. After they have left, the stylist can explain what happened from their point of view. If the stylist truly made a mistake, apologies are a good idea. In this case, the manager might comp (not charge for) the haircut. Everybody endures difficult situations with clients. The important thing is to handle them with grace.

Part of your job is to make sure clients understand the upkeep required for that gorgeous style they saw in a magazine. Will that color fade oddly? Are their roots going to need frequent touch ups? Will they need lots of product to achieve that look?

Your first job teaches the importance of good work habits. New stylists and barbers learn what they need to do to be on time and to look their best. They'll learn to determine when they really need to call out and how to do it properly. You'll learn the importance of good customer service and being polite and friendly to everyone. You'll learn to be part of a team—to work hard and pitch in when people need help, and to keep your area clean and stocked. All this makes your boss's job easier and makes them more inclined to give you a good review or recommendation.

A word about bosses: Most want their workers to enjoy and succeed in their jobs. After all, happy employees attract happy customers. However, if you have a difficult boss, consider your choices. Can you quit? If you work for a large chain of salons, check out their website or your employee handbook to see if there's anyone in human resources you can speak to. If not, decide how you want to look back on handling the situation, and do that. The same is true of a job you dislike for other reasons. Determine if you can reasonably quit or if you need to stick it out for a while longer. In that case, set a timeframe for when you can seek a new job. That will give you something to look forward to.

Many barbers and hairstylists love their first job. But there comes a time when they want to earn more and challenge themselves with a new position. Or maybe they've completed additional classes in a different cosmetology art, and they need to move to a larger salon that offers that treatment.

WHAT'S NEXT?

With adequate experience, workers can advance from their entry-level job. They can do this at their present place of employment, by advancing from an assistant to a stylist, for instance. Or they can look elsewhere. If you decide to move to a different salon, have your new job lined up before you leave. Always make a professional exit, even if you aren't happy at a job. Two weeks' notice is the standard in most industries.

Perhaps you might want to work at a more upscale salon, where you'll make more money per hair appointment. Or you may choose to work in a spa, which typically offers more services, including facials and massages, and requires its hairstylists to have more experience. Competition for high-end salon and spa work is steep. Job seekers will need to pound the pavement again, following the same steps they took to find their first job. But years of experience under your belt will set you apart from other candidates.

Spas tend to offer upscale services such as massage therapy and advanced skin treatments as well as hair and nail services. You may need to take more specialized cosmetology classes in addition to your salon experience to join the staff of a spa.

SPAS AND SALONS ON CRUISE SHIPS

Maybe you're looking to escape from the place where you grew up. Literally. If traveling is one of your big dreams, you might consider a job on board a cruise ship. Many cruise ships offer full-scale salon and spa services. You'll need to be licensed, the same as if you work in a salon on land and have an excellent command of written and spoken English. You'll work a tough schedule for demanding clients, but you'll get to see the world, earn a competitive salary and/or commissions, plus gratuities, and not have any major living expenses.

If you work on a cruise ship, you have no commute. Housing and medical care are part of your compensation. Plus, you get amazing views!

Having a clientele is also a selling point to salons. For stylists and barbers working on commission, it's also essential to their income. If a stylist has an established clientele, half of those customers will likely follow them to a new salon if it isn't too far away.

But is the stylist allowed to take those clients from the present salon? Right now, it depends on which state they're doing business in. Some salons include a "non-compete" clause in contracts offered to hairstylists or barbers. This states that upon quitting the job, the employee can't work as a hairstylist or barber within a certain distance (say 10 or 20 miles [16 or 32 kilometers]) for a certain amount of time (perhaps a year). These agreements are meant to protect employers from losing clients that they invested advertising money to bring in.

However, some states are outlawing these agreements. Currently California, Minnesota, North Dakota, and Oklahoma prohibit non-compete agreements, and New York is in the process of enacting a similar law. The Federal Trade Commission (FTC) is also looking into the matter.

This barber shop looks like it's discovered its perfect niche clientele.

Q&A WITH A SALON OWNER

Here are some words of wisdom from an experienced stylist and salon owner:

How did you know you wanted to be a hairstylist?
I was always interested in doing my friends' and sisters' hair and makeup. When it came time to decide on a college, my interest grew more intense. I ended up going to college for one semester and then decided to follow my true passion for hair.

What was your first job as a hairstylist?
My first job was an assistant position at a well-known salon and spa. I worked there for one year.

What was your next career step after that?
I went to a booth-rental salon. It was a bit of a risk because I did not have many clients, but I knew it was what I wanted. So, I worked very, very hard at becoming a booked stylist.

How did you come to own your own salon?
My husband and I bought a property a bit over a year ago with the intention of opening my own salon. I had worked for someone else in a booth-rental salon for over five years and was ready for the next step.

What does it take to be a good hairstylist?
It takes a lot of determination. If you want to be good at something, you can be if you work hard enough at it. A good stylist has to keep up with hair trends and

training. You need to make sure your clients come first and do whatever it may be to please them. At the same time, you need to steer them in the right direction to make sure they are looking their best!

What is your advice for those who would like to own their own salon?
My advice would be to be organized and professional, and make sure you have the best people working for you.

MARKETING YOURSELF

Some barbers and hairstylists work at salons in malls which have a constant flow of customers. Others work for chains or big-name salons that have their own marketing departments. Of course, if you work in a resort or on a cruise ship, you have a captive audience. But most barbers and stylists will have to market themselves.

Marketing and building clientele are ongoing processes. People move. They go to college. They try new things. Stylists and barbers need to replace old business with new business. Here are some ways to do that:

- **Give clients two business cards.** Ask them to give one to a friend. If the friend returns with it, you'll give both the client and friend a discounted haircut. Or design a punch card—perhaps every 10th cut is discounted. Big box office supply stores and online printing services produce professional-quality business cards and other swag for reasonable prices.

- **Get involved with the local chamber of commerce and neighborhood business association.** This is a great way to network with potential clients. Consider having a print ad in a local event program or donating a gift certificate to a raffle.

- **Host a charity event, such as a cut-a-thon, in which hairstylists donate a day of haircuts.** The people getting a haircut donate a set amount to a charity. This helps the charity and brings new clients into the salon. You can also participate in an event providing free haircuts for people experiencing homelessness.

- **Cross promote.** If a nail salon is next door, give the manicurist some of your business cards and take some of theirs. You can both pass them out to customers.

- **Collect email addresses and send out a newsletter.** Newsletters can feature new style trends and products, reminding customers to return. There are inexpensive online services to manage mailing lists.

- **Send out holiday and birthday greetings.** You can do this online or via the postal service. Consider adding a coupon to birthday cards.

- **Use social media, such as Facebook and Instagram.** Create a fan page on Facebook for people to join. Instagram is a great platform for sharing photos of your work.

- **Target specific clients.** Younger clients are a growing customer demographic. Around prom season, advertise promotions, such as 10 percent off updos if two friends come in together. If there is a college near your salon, you may be able to attract students who haven't yet found a hairstylist in town. The school newspaper or online message board may be a good place to advertise.

- **Run monthly sales promotions.** Advertise these in your shop window, or if you can afford it, in a newspaper or other publication. And of course, post them on your social media accounts.

- **Don't limit yourself.** You should be able to do all kinds of hair: curly and straight, coarse and fine, thick and thin, natural and treated. If there's something you don't know how to do, take a class and learn.

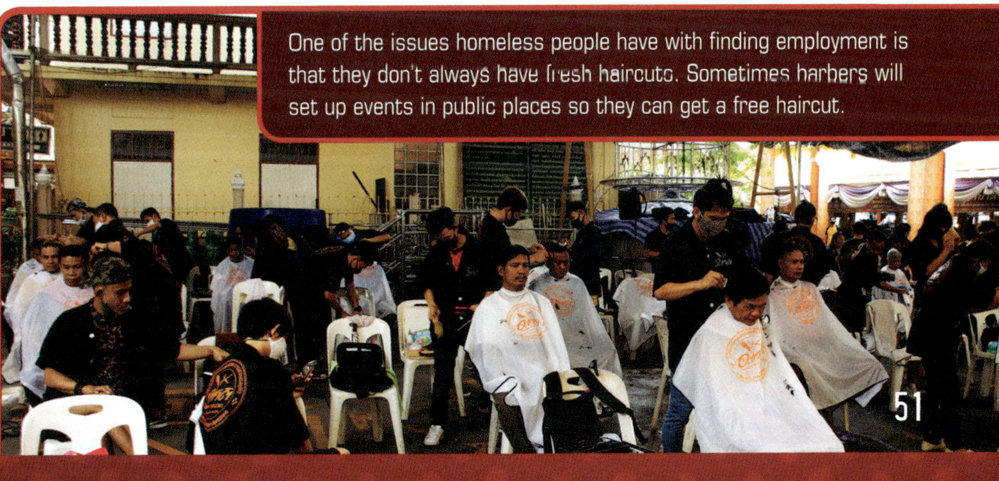

One of the issues homeless people have with finding employment is that they don't always have fresh haircuts. Sometimes barbers will set up events in public places so they can get a free haircut.

Once you have some experience as a professional barber or hairstylist, you'll have a better idea of what options are open to you. Maybe dealing directly with clients all day and not having to do any sort of management or bookkeeping is exactly what you want to do.

But maybe you have a different vision. Perhaps you want to use your hairstyling experience as a springboard to something bigger, such as a career in movies, theater, or fashion. Or maybe you have an idea for a fabulous spa or salon of your own. And someday, standing on your feet all day might not be as appealing. Maybe then you'd like to teach or sell salon products.

NATURAL AND ETHNIC HAIR

Annie Turnbo Malone (1869–1957) was one of the first entrepreneurs to create and sell a hair care product designed especially for African American hair. While you may not recognize her name, you've probably heard of Madam C. J. Walker (1867–1919). Walker started out as one of Malone's sales agents, but later developed and marketed her own hair care products.

The Guinness Book of World Records recognizes Walker as America's first self-made female millionaire. The National Trust for Historic Preservation designated her restored home, Villa Lewaro, in Irvington, New York, as a National Historic Landmark in 1976.

Today, major cosmetology textbooks cover natural and ethnic hair, and beauty schools include it in the curriculum. Students learn to care for and style all sorts of hair. A client shouldn't have to seek out a special salon—any trained hairdresser should be able to style their hair.

Walker's Irvington home was a gathering place for many prominent figures of the Harlem Renaissance.

CHAPTER FOUR

HAIRSTYLIST, BARBER, OR BUSINESS OWNER?

The history of hair care goes back to the earliest human civilizations. People were aware of the connection between looking good and feeling good long before it was recognized by medical and mental health professionals. They knew they felt better if they were clean and neatly groomed, and they were happier if they looked good.

The art of hairdressing goes back to those early civilizations. Ancient Egyptians wore weaves and wigs. Ancient Greek women dyed their hair red with henna or sprinkled gold powder on it. In Rome, elaborately curled long hair—often dyed blond—was the style. The enslaved Romans that did hair, ornatrices, were some of the first trained hairstylists.

In early America, women wore their hair long and styled it themselves. In the 18th century, women wore caps on a daily basis. Fashionable women might wear elaborate hairstyles or wigs for special occasions. Gentlemen or those who followed a profession would wear wigs to differentiate themselves from workmen, who wore caps or hats for work.

In the 19th century, magazines such as *Godey's Lady's Book* printed fashion news and illustrations. Women across America would copy the styles they read about or saw in the fashion plates.

Then, in the early 1900s, women began opening hair salons. The need for salons grew in the 1920s, when the popular bob hairstyle required a professional's expertise. At first, some women went to barbers for bobs. Eventually, they opted for beauty shops, where they could also get permanents and hair coloring, manicures, and facials. With the growth of salons grew the need for beauty schools.

Both salons and schools were segregated at the time. Although segregation has been illegal for a long time, many salons still serve either a white or Black clientele. In some cases, this is because of neighborhood demographics and personal choice. However, cosmetology schools are trying to change this by training students to do all kinds of hair. They're teaching that hair doesn't differ so greatly between ethnic groups that they have to go to separate salons and barbershops.

Careers in cosmetology offered both Black and white women more independence and creative license than many other careers available. Besides Annie Turnbo Malone and Madam C.J. Walker who pioneered African American hair care, the permanent wave machine was invented by Marjorie Joyner, the granddaughter of an enslaved woman.

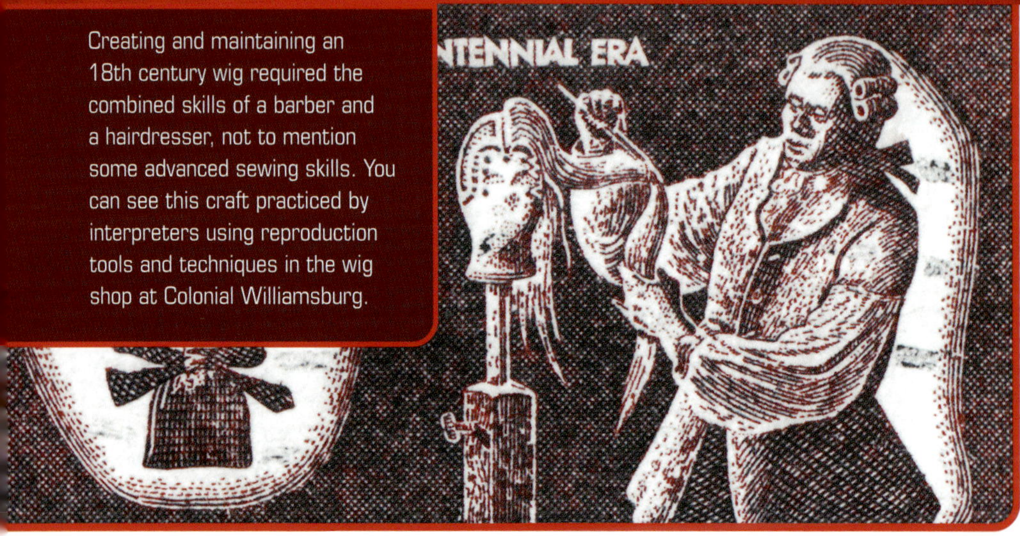

Creating and maintaining an 18th century wig required the combined skills of a barber and a hairdresser, not to mention some advanced sewing skills. You can see this craft practiced by interpreters using reproduction tools and techniques in the wig shop at Colonial Williamsburg.

MARJORIE JOYNER AND HER PERM MACHINE

Marjorie Stewart Joyner (1896–1994) was an African American cosmetology pioneer. She's best remembered for inventing and patenting the permanent wave machine in 1928. Joyner was the first African American to graduate from the A.B. Molar Beauty School in Chicago in 1916. She later enrolled in Madam C.J. Walker's school to learn how to style African American hair.

Joyner opened her own salon, then eventually became a vice president in Madam C.J. Walker's company. Joyner served as the national adviser to Walker's 200 cosmetology schools. Although her permanent wave system was a great success, the rights were owned by Walker's company, so she didn't see any financial return from her invention.

In 1987, the Smithsonian exhibited a replica of Joyner's salon.

If you've seen movies set in the 1950s and early 1960s such as *Hairspray* or *The Help*—yes, ladies really did wear those big, poufy bouffant hairdos. Generally, those hairstyles required a weekly trip to the beauty parlor. Hair would be washed, and curled, then the client would need to sit under the hairdryer, then their hair would be styled—and sprayed so it wouldn't move in a stiff breeze.

Then, in the early 1960s, Vidal Sassoon created the five-point bob and other low-maintenance styles. Women no longer needed to go to the salon weekly. However, their "wash and wear" cuts required regular professional trims. They also continued to see stylists for specialty services, such as highlighting, perms, and relaxing treatments.

Ladies in the 50s and 60s expected lengthy beauty parlor visits, including time spent sitting under the hair drier.

Through the years, the styles and even the politics of hair have changed. Fancy, high maintenance styles were fine when most women stayed at home, but the simple bob was much better for professional women. But one thing has stayed the same: When it comes to their hair, many women trust only the pros.

Being a professional requires skillful hairstyling, which stylists learn through schooling and practice. It also requires excellent business skills, including knowing how to negotiate salary and fees.

GETTING PAID

No matter how much you love your job, eventually you're going to feel like you should be paid more. If you work for a large company, there may be a schedule in place—a small raise after your first 90 days (or other specified probationary period), and then a review and raise every year on the anniversary of your hire. And of course, if you're promoted within the company, that should be accompanied by a raise. Large companies often conduct competitive wage surveys and will sometimes increase all their employees' pay so it's on a par with similar local businesses.

However, if you work for a small shop, you may need to approach the idea of a raise a bit differently. You may need to talk to your boss about earning more than your entry-level wage. You should always say why you deserve a raise (for example: "I've brought in x number of customers in the past six months, and I average x number of appointments a day") and not why you need it (for example: "I just moved into a more expensive apartment"). If the boss says no, employees can ask what goals they need to meet in order to get a raise. They should set a time to renegotiate.

When working on commission or renting a booth, workers can give themselves a raise by increasing prices every couple of years. Clients should be told tactfully when rates go up. Also, rates shouldn't be raised too high or at the wrong time (such as when a property tax increase has just been announced, or a large company that provides lots of local jobs is shutting down their big facility in your town). Stylists and barbers should be sensitive to their customers' need for affordable hairstyling, but they shouldn't sell themselves short either.

Vidal Sassoon's stylish, low maintenance haircuts and Mary Quant's miniskirts suited busy career women in the late 1960s.

Another way to increase income is through product sales. Stylists who hope to boost their income this way should practice the art of soft selling. Tell the clients what you are using in their hair and why. Then, put the products in a basket at the front desk in case they are interested in buying them. Don't push the sale. Be sure to choose products in a reasonable price range for the neighborhood.

Eventually, as you gain more business experience and a bigger clientele, you might decide to go into business for yourself. This is a common choice for cosmetologists. About half are self-employed—either as booth renters or salon owners. This is a big step, and you'll want to do lots of research before committing to it.

YE OLDE BARBERSHOP

Like hairdressing, the art of barbering dates to the earliest civilizations. Barbers cared for members of the Egyptian nobility, trimming hair, shaving, and applying makeup. By the time of the Greek and Roman civilizations, barbers also performed dentistry and minor surgery.

Throughout the Middle Ages, barbers practiced major surgery such as amputations and bloodletting—a process of removing blood, which people at the time thought cured sicknesses. The word barber was first used in the 14th century.

Then in the 1500s, King Henry VIII of England forbid barber-surgeons from doing anything more than pulling teeth and bloodletting. By the end of the 1700s, barbers had given up dentistry and bloodletting and focused on making wigs, which were popular among men at the time. As wigs fell out of fashion, barbershops rose again. During and after the American Civil War, they were a place to gather. At the time, barbershops, like most businesses, were segregated. In African American communities, patrons would sometimes sing together. This style became known as barbershop quartet.

Today, many men continue to gather at the neighborhood barbershops. For older men, the neighborhood barbershop is still a place to socialize. Younger men might prefer an upscale barbershop and or chain where barbers are up on the latest looks. Traditional neighborhood shops are being handed down to new generations of barbers. In a nod to history, the red-and-white pole symbolizes the blood-stained rags that barber-surgeons would wash and hang out to dry.

The idea of a barbershop quartet isn't something Hollywood made up. People used to gather to sing recreationally. The Barbershop Harmony Society, based in Nashville, works to preserve this musical tradition.

Some men enjoy upscale facial services. Take a look around your community and see what services are offered in neighborhood shops.

Today, barbers are trained to cut, trim, and style hair and beards, as well as to do color and perms, but many just cut hair. With the dawn of the safety razor and personal electric shavers, shaving is less common. Barbering can be a solid career for the same reasons that hairstyling can be. Men want to look their best, and they turn to barbers for a good cut. Some men get their hair cut every month or, for a very short cut, every two weeks. Some men choose to wear a beard as a matter of personal style and want it maintained in a particular way. Finally, men are often loyal to their barber and barbershop. They may return to the same place their whole lives and bring their sons, too.

Often, when barbers start out, they look for an open chair at a neighborhood or chain barbershop. They work for wages or salary in the beginning, rather than renting a chair. It's good to get a solid understanding of the trade before adding in business operations. Eventually, many barbers go into business for themselves, either as a chair renter or as a barbershop owner. Before taking this step, they should have a good understanding of things such as taxes, supplies, and payroll.

When barbers own their own business, they usually also cut hair. This requires them to handle the business end—accounting, purchasing, inventory, industry compliance, and human relations work—in addition to the hours they spend working with clients. This is something to keep in mind before going into business for yourself.

The outlook for barbers is good. For years, upscale salons and spas catered to a mostly female clientele. Now, upscale barbershops or grooming lounges are offering men the luxury of spas with the masculinity of barbershops. Some offer facial treatment or manicures. Sports-themed barbershops, which advertise sports programming in a men-only atmosphere, and other chains are also breaking into the market. These places will create jobs and create competition. The neighborhood shop owners will need to work hard to bring in new clients and retain the old.

INTERVIEW WITH A MASTER BARBER

Just like men can be hairdressers, women can be barbers. A master barber is one who's practiced their trade for at least seven years or been issued a certificate from their state. Maura Scali-Sheahan is a master barber and an author.

How did you decide to be a barber?
I wanted to work with hair, but the beauty salon environment did not appeal to me, so I arranged to visit my father's barber. Within 15 minutes of observing the barbers at work, I knew what I wanted to do.

Where did you attend barber school?
With the help of my father's barber, I was the first female allowed to enroll at the Chicago Barber College. The school was segregated by race, and once I enrolled, by sex, too. They assigned me a chair in the corner away from all the men.

What was your first barbershop job?
While still in school, I worked for the same barber who had helped me get into school. I did men's manicures chair-side, which means I did their nails while they had their hair cut. Once I graduated, I cut hair at the same barbershop.

What was your next career move?
I managed a shop in Georgia, then went back to Illinois and opened my own shop. I began writing articles for the *National Beauty School Journal*, relocated

to Florida, and accepted a job at Florida Community College to start up their barbering program. An opportunity to revise the barbering textbook for Milady Publishing quickly followed. I've trained educators and helped barber schools strengthen their programs. I've also served as the director of education for Barbers International. Combining interests and passions has led to great things and, as with any field, barbering has unlimited possibilities.

BEING YOUR OWN BOSS

Many hairstylists and barbers work for themselves. This is a big step that requires a lot of thought and planning. Before striking out on your own, you want to have solid experience with your trade. You want at least one job on your résumé and a network of both clients and professional contacts.

The first step toward self-employment is often booth rental. This is a growing trend. It benefits hairstylists and barbers because they get their money on the day of service instead of waiting two weeks for a paycheck. It benefits salons because they do not have to pay taxes on tips earned by stylists (which go to the stylist, not the salon). It also requires less hands-on management.

In booth rental, stylists or barbers pay monthly rent to the salon or shop for space. If they sell products, they acquire their own sales tax number. They don't receive a paycheck with taxes already deducted. They keep track of income, tips, and expenses, and file their own taxes. Instead of

Sometimes, older men grow beards because they take prescription blood thinners. This means they can bleed very badly from a small nick while shaving. This is why it's important to know your clients and listen when they speak.

getting a refund at tax time, they must pay. This is the sort of thing you need professional advice on. Before leaving a salaried or hourly position, take a seminar on self-employment or be prepared to hire an accountant or tax adviser.

Workers who rent a booth are self-employed. They can't be required to work specific hours or days or to adhere to a non-compete agreement (in places where those are legal). Before entering into a booth rental, stylists and barbers should understand what they are responsible for and what the salon does. Will the salon owner market the salon, for instance, or are renters responsible for their own marketing?

Rather than renting a booth, some workers opt to work at home. This may work if their existing clientele lives close to their home, and if they have a quiet, clean work area available. The benefits of working from home are that there is no added rent, a percentage of rent or mortgage payments is tax deductible, work hours are flexible, and there is no commute. This can be a good option for a parent or caregiver. The disadvantages are that some clients prefer a salon atmosphere, and there may be distractions at home that make work difficult. You also need to be aware if there are any restrictions on commercial activity in your neighborhood and things like available parking.

Renting a booth or working from home teaches workers how to order supplies, keep books, and market themselves. Supplies are generally cheaper in bulk, but if you work alone you don't need as much. So, do you pay higher prices for smaller quantities, find a place to store supplies, or find some middle ground, like shopping at really good sales? Marketing requires time, attention, and money. You'll need dedicated social media accounts that are kept up to date. How about a website or print marketing? Those who would like to do that on a larger scale, while also managing employees and a workspace, might want to own or manage a salon or barbershop.

Whether it's a small salon or barbershop, a large full-service spa, or a new barbershop or salon franchise, owners need business know-how. They might take online courses specializing in the cosmetology business, take general business courses, or work under a successful owner or manager. Getting a job as an assistant manager before going into business for yourself might be a wise move.

If you're in business for yourself, you need to think about how and where your supplies will be stored. A local beauty supply shop may be a good compromise between buying large, heavy boxes of supplies from a distributor or paying full price per bottle at a grocery or drug store.

Prospective owners will need to watch for opportunities. If they want to open a new salon in a certain neighborhood, they'll watch for rental space. In this case, they may need to remodel the area to fit the salon or barbershop's needs. This is where you want to check out your network. Do you know a general contractor, plumber, or electrician? The space you rent will need to have a storage room, space for some sort of reception desk, and however many workstations you plan to include. Are there enough sinks? How about restrooms? Do you want to share with your clients, or will you need two? How is the electrical setup?

Now think about your business plan. If you're planning to open a salon that offers high-end services in a neighborhood full of trendy boutiques, you'll probably do well. But if it's a working-class area full of families with small children, you might want to think about how you can tailor your ideas to best serve the community—and make money.

An alternative is to buy a salon already in operation. In that case, the shape of the business should be assessed. Does it have a steady stream of customers? Will the hairstylists stay under new ownership? Is the equipment working? Does the building require work? Even if it doesn't require renovations, there's always advertising and rebranding, which will cost money. For workers wanting to manage a salon or franchise, their best bet is probably to get a job there and work their way up.

A strip mall can be a good choice for a new salon or barbershop. People already come there for other things, there's plenty of parking, and a certain amount of maintenance is probably included in the rent.

The responsibilities of an owner or manager include hiring, training, and managing associates. In any leadership position, it's important to keep employees happy. That's especially true with hairstyling and barbering. Customers are loyal to their stylists, not the shop. If workers leave, the customers go with them.

On the business side, owners and managers handle merchandising, bookkeeping, and marketing. They make sure employee paychecks and rent are paid on time. They need to keep track of things such as professional certifications and health code permits. That's a lot for one person, so it can be a good idea to have a partner. Sometimes one partner manages the employees and customer service while the other handles the business side.

When starting up a salon or barbershop, coming up with a name can be fun. Will it have a cheesy, pun name, a stylish name, or an old-school name? Setting up and decorating the shop and determining its atmosphere is also exciting. In a local setting, introduce yourself to your neighbors. Perhaps you might offer a grand opening discount to employees of local businesses to generate some referrals. You could also consider joining a local business organization. Choosing colors and logos is fun! You'll probably also want to purchase some cool giveaways such as emery boards with your business information.

Starting a business isn't all about picking balloons and hanging banners. There are a lot of details and hidden costs to deal with. Owners need to work out things like:

- Rental contracts (Read the fine print!)
- Remodeling expenses (Always more than you planned for.)
- Financing
- Staffing (How many days/hours do you plan to be open? How many people do you need total?)
- Employee benefits (Do your research and find out what's competitive in your area.)
- Legal matters
- Permits, permits, permits
- Maintenance and cleaning (Do you need to hire someone to shovel the sidewalk in winter? How is garbage collected? What about washing the windows?)

Business ownership is a huge commitment of time, energy, and money, but it's rewarding to provide jobs and a service to the neighborhood.

Remember that network we keep mentioning? Do you know any artists or interior designers? They can help you achieve the cool image you have in mind for your new business!

CHAPTER FIVE

CAREERS OUTSIDE THE SALON

However much you love doing hair, there may come a time when you don't want to stand on your feet behind the chair all day—not to mention sweeping up and washing all those towels afterwards! When that time comes, you'll have lots of options. One is to work for a hair product company. These companies develop new shampoos, conditioners, hair colors, wigs, extensions, and other products for men and women. Jobs for one of these companies can provide an opportunity for travel and a more flexible schedule. Here are some jobs in this field:

- **Product sales representative.** Sales representatives may work for the product company or a local or national distributor. They might sell products to beauty shops or direct to the general public. Some might work at a brand name counter inside a bigger store. These companies hire licensed cosmetologists since they are familiar with the products and the salon business. Sales people typically work on salary and commission. To break into the field, stylists can network with their salon's product reps. They can inquire about the field and let the reps know they are interested. Stylists can also go to trade shows and talk to representatives there. These meetings could lead to a job. Stylists should also pay attention to which products work best and choose a brand they're passionate about. Enthusiasm for a brand shows in a job interview.

- **Product educator/platform artist.** To promote hair products, educators travel to salons and trade shows to train stylists. This is an exciting option if you love travel and love to be the center of attention! Platform artists demonstrate how to use the products to achieve the latest styles. To break into this field, stylists can assist another platform artist. They can also gain experience by entering hair competitions. To succeed as a platform artist, stylists need to be good teachers and be able to project ideas confidently to a large audience. They work with models and organize a backstage staff for the demonstration. Be aware that most trade shows happen over weekends, so that's when you'll be working. Typically, platform artists aren't full-time employees. They freelance while working at a salon.

Trade shows are a great way to connect with other beauty professionals and learn about new products.

NURSING HOMES AND RETIREMENT COMMUNITIES

There's a proven link between looking good and feeling good. For this reason, retirement communities, assisted living facilities, and nursing homes often have their own salon, spa, or barbershop. These facilities can range from a full-service spa in large facilities to a visiting hairdresser in small ones.

Sometimes these services have very practical reasons. An elderly person might have trouble raising their arms or have difficulty standing in the shower long enough to wash their own hair, so it's safer to have it washed by a hairdresser while sitting in a chair. Hairdressers and barbers are also trained to know what a healthy scalp looks like, so they sometimes spot things that should be checked by a doctor or dermatologist.

For elderly residents, visiting the hairdresser is a fun social occasion. Working in this type of setting can have a positive influence on older peoples' lives.

Even residents who are confused or unsettled enjoy having their hair combed or picking out a new color of nail polish.

GIVING BACK TO THE COMMUNITY

Hairstylists and barbers are an integral part of any community. At some point in your career, you may decide you want to contribute to your community in a different way. One way could be becoming an educator. Teaching the next generation of hairstylists and barbers entails writing lesson plans; teaching hairstyling, safety, and hygiene; and observing students to ensure they have learned the techniques. Becoming a cosmetology teacher requires additional training. Milady breaks this into three levels or certificates. You already know how to style hair—now you need to learn teaching techniques. In addition to teaching in the classroom or lab during the day, you'll have evening homework to grade. Those who pursue this field find it rewarding to see their students master the art of hairstyling. In addition to teachers, cosmetology and barber schools need program directors and curriculum developers.

Textbook companies—primarily Milady and Pivot Point—hire cosmetologists and barbers to write the textbooks used by schools. You can gain experience for this by first writing articles for barber and hairstylist trade magazines.

Another way for cosmetologists to give back to their community is by working with an organization that helps cancer patients or other people with medical conditions that impact their appearance. Many cancer centers across America have boutiques that include wig fitting and styling. This career allows hairstylists to help cancer patients—whether men, women, or children—feel better by looking their best.

Some stylists and barbers may want to broaden their horizons without leaving the salon. Volunteering is a great way to do that. For cosmetologists, there are lots of volunteer opportunities. Look Good... Feel Better is a service that helps cancer patients look their best. Locks of Love and Wigs for Kids are organizations that encourage people to donate their hair, which is used for wigs for children who suffer hair loss. Cut It Out trains hairstylists to recognize signs of domestic violence and encourage clients to get help. Through the Black Barbershop Health Outreach Program, barbershops that cater to an African American clientele can offer diabetes and high blood pressure screenings to their clients. To date, they've provided health screenings to more than 30,000 African American men.

Both beauticians and barbers are needed by nursing homes and hospice programs to give the residents haircuts or shaves. Even sick or confused residents feel better when they get their hair done. First, it cleans the scalp, making them feel better physically. Second, it boosts their self-esteem. Their family tells them they look better. A positive outlook is a definite step toward healing!

TODAY'S CELEBRITY HAIRDRESSERS

KIM KIMBLE	Hairstylist to stars, including Beyoncé, with more than half a million Instagram followers.

TED GIBSON	Star of *What Not to Wear*. His celebrity haircuts cost as much as $2,000.
JEN ATKIN	Stylist to the Kardashians, the *New York Times* calls her the world's most influential hairstylist.

WORKING IN PRINT OR FILM

Maybe you've always dreamed of doing something glamorous—theater, film, or magazine work. Of course, to produce the glam the general public sees requires a lot of hard work behind the scenes, and a good bit of luck if you want to work with top models or big stars.

Print stylists work for magazines or catalogs. Fashion magazine work is considered the most prestigious of these. It involves styling hair for models appearing in publications such as *Vogue* or *Elle*.

Every career starts somewhere. You might get your first experience working on catalog shoots, most likely with models who are also just starting out.

Stylists are typically freelance. They might work in a salon and moonlight as a print stylist until they get enough consistent work as a stylist. Typically, they get started in the business by assisting a stylist. Eventually, they'll have enough experience to strike out on their own.

Remember, there's more to the print industry than the big fashion magazines. Catalogs, magazines, and local advertisements are full of photographs, and all those people needed a hairstylist for the shoot.

INTERVIEW WITH INDIA GENTILE

When you've worked your way up to the big-name fashion magazines, you'll need an agent. Here's some advice from a Hollywood stylists' agent.

Describe your job as an agent.
It is managing every aspect of an artist's career—from booking travel to negotiating rates, updating their portfolios, generating work, and establishing them in the world of beauty.

What are some of the most interesting projects you've worked on?
One of my hairstylists was chosen as the key hairstylist for Sarah Jessica Parker for *Sex and the City*.

What skills are required for your job?
Competence! Patience, balancing all the artists you represent. Being compassionate yet authoritative.

What experience do hairstylists need prior to becoming a freelance stylist for magazines, television, or film?
You need expertise at cutting and styling hair, as well as having basic knowledge of applying wigs and extensions. I would also recommend assisting one of your favorite editorial hairstylists for two to four years. Then build your book with tear sheets and when it gets to the point of you not being able to manage your jobs and work together, find an agency.

What skills or talents does it take to be a hairstylist for a magazine?
To work for a magazine like *Vogue*, you need 10 to 15 years of experience. For a less-established magazine, you may need only a few. You need to be a confident hairstylist and a good collaborator. You have to keep up with the trends, not just in hair, but also in fashion.

Print stylists build their reputation by styling hair for models appearing in magazine fashion spreads. This is called editorial work. Next, they seek work as stylists for models appearing in advertisements. Advertising work pays much better, but the advertisers want to see editorial photos first. The best cities for print stylists include New York, Los Angeles, Miami, and Chicago, but also smaller cities with strong advertising agencies, such as Kansas City. However, remember that there are many layers to any profession, and you might find local work.

Stylists interested in being print stylists can attend classes at well-known salons, such as Bumble and Bumble and Cutler Salon in New York. There are also programs designed for editorial stylists. Working at a prestigious salon in their hometown is also a good stepping stone to a career in print hairstyling. Meanwhile, workers should study fashion magazines, learn who the key stylists are, and understand the style trends.

To find work or an agent, stylists need a portfolio. This should contain photos of a variety of hairstyles they've done. To create these photos, stylists can work with a photographer and model who are also building portfolios. This is another area where networking comes into play. If stylists have samples of work that have been in a magazine (tear sheets), they should include those, too. When the book is put together, the stylist can email an agent stating that he or she is interested in assisting a stylist. The stylist should send a résumé and ask if he or she can send a portfolio. Once the stylist has gained experience, he or she can ask the agent for representation.

To keep being hired for jobs, stylists need to be talented, quick, and professional. They need to be on time, listen to what is needed, and, even if everyone else is acting stressed out, keep their cool.

Starting out, print stylists don't make much money. However, after several years, they can earn a steady or even lucrative income.

Other types of stylists work in film and television. These jobs might include being the stylist for a television show, advertisement, or movie, or for a particular actor. (Top actors usually have their own hairstylists on set.) Stylists are also needed for fashion runway shows, plays, ballets, and live television programs—and these events happen everywhere. Stylists can break into this field in the same way they would break into print media. If your heart is set on the big leagues, you might need to relocate to New York or Los Angeles, though many ads are shot elsewhere. For a portfolio, you'll want to include a wider range of hairstyles, including wigs and period hairstyles. To work in Hollywood, you may also need to join the Makeup Artists and Hair Stylists Guild (part of the International Alliance of theatrical Stage Employees Motion Picture Technicians, Artist and Allied Crafts of the United States and Canada [IATSE]).

Keep in mind there are levels to every profession. Ads on your local cable station probably weren't filmed in New York City or Los Angeles. There's probably a community theater and a professional theater in your area. You might be able to do the kind of work you dream of without leaving home, or you might gain contacts and experience that help you achieve your big dreams.

On smaller projects, you might do both hair and makeup.

10 GREAT QUESTIONS TO ASK A HAIRSTYLIST

Here are some questions you can ask a hairstylist. If there are multiple shops nearby, try to visit a hair salon, spa, and a barbershop for different perspectives.

1. Did you go to cosmetology school or college?
2. Can you recommend a school nearby? About how much will it cost?
3. Did you take extra business classes?
4. Do you have a favorite style? Why did you choose it?
5. Are you part of a staff or do you rent a chair?
6. Are there any books you recommend I read? Industry blogs or magazines that are worth following?
7. Has your job changed since the COVID-19 pandemic?
8. Did you go back to school or to trade shows to learn about new styles and techniques?
9. Are you also trained to do makeup and nails?
10. Do you want to own your own shop or do you like being able to concentrate on hair?

What other questions can you think of?

Working as a hairstylist lets you earn a living doing fun creative work that makes your clients feel good about themselves.

GLOSSARY

aesthetician: A cosmetologist that focuses on skin care services, such as facials.

agent: A person who represents an artist, such as a hair-stylist, by booking jobs and negotiating contract and financial matters.

beautician: A worker trained in the cosmetology arts. Today, "cosmetologist" is the more common term.

beauty parlor: A business that offers beauty services, such as hairstyling. Today, it is commonly known as a hair salon.

bloodletting: The practice of removing blood from a patient to cure or prevent illness.

cosmetologist: A worker trained in hairstyling, manicures, pedicures, waxing, facials, and makeup art.

freelance: Describes a worker whose services are sold to buyers on a job-by-job basis.

grooming lounge: A salon or spa specializing in men's services, such as haircuts and shaves.

hairstylist: A cosmetologist specializing in hair care.

Milady: A company that publishes cosmetology and barbering textbooks.

nail technician: A cosmetologist that specializes in manicures and pedicures.

Pivot Point: A company that publishes cosmetology textbooks.

platform artist: An artist that represents hair product companies by demonstrating hairstyling techniques using those products.

portfolio: A collection of samples of a person's work, such as photographs of hairstyles a hairstylist has done.

print stylist: A stylist that does hair for models appearing in magazine photo spreads, print ads, or catalogs.

salon: A business that offers beauty services, such as hairstyling.

spa: A business that offers beauty and relaxation services.

tear sheets: Clippings from magazines that show an artist's work.

upscale: Appealing to affluent customers.

FOR MORE INFORMATION

ALLIED BEAUTY ASSOCIATION

BOX 30068 Cityside Postal Outlet
Mississauga, ON
Canada
(905) 568-0158
Website: abacanada.com
Facebook and Instagram: @ABACanada
The ABA represents Canadian beauty professionals.

AMERICAN BARBER ASSOCIATION

P.O. Box 11661
Shorewood, WI 53211
(929) 399-6233
Website: americanbarber.org
Facebook: @BarberUSA
Instagram: @barbersusa
ABA is a leading source of information and education for the barber industry.

ASSOCIATED HAIR PROFESSIONALS

25188 Genesee Trail Road
Suite 200
Golden, CO 80401
(800) 575-4642
Website: www.associatedhairprofessionals.com
Facebook and Instagram: @ahphair
AHP is a professional organization for hairstylists and barbers. They offer educational, professional, and community support for hair professionals.

BEAUTYCOUNCIL

P.O. Box 16002
North Vancouver, BC V7J 3S9
Canada
(604) 871-0222
Website: beautycouncil.ca
BeautyCouncil is a community of salon, spa, and barber professionals located in western Canada.

INTERNATIONAL ALLIANCE OF THEATRICAL STAGE EMPLOYEES MOVING PICTURE TECHNICIANS ARTISTS AND ALLIED CRAFTS OF THE UNITED STATES ITS TERRITORIES AND CANADA

207 W. 25th St, 4th Fl.
New York, NY 10001
(212) 730-1770
Website: iatse.net
Facebook and Instagram: @iatse
IATSE is the labor union that represents stylists and makeup artists who work in the entertainment industry.

MADAM C J WALKER

Website: madamcjwalker.com
The official website of Madam C.J. Walker contains media and biographical information.

MILADY

5 Maxwell Dr.
Clifton Park, NY 12065
(866) 848-5143
Website: milady.com
Milady publishes one of the most widely used cosmetology textbooks.

NATIONAL ASSOCIATION OF BARBER BOARDS OF AMERICA

9252 San Jose Blvd. #3703
Jacksonville, FL 32257
(888) 338-0101
Website: nationalbarberboards.com
The National Association of Barber Boards of America is an organization dedicated to maintaining professional standards and policies in the barbering industry.

PIVOT POINT

8725 W. Higgins Road, Suite 700
Chicago, IL 60631
(847) 866-0500
Website: pivot-point.com
Facebook: @PivotPointInternational
Instagram: @pivotpointintl
Pivot Point publishes one of the most widely used cosmetology textbooks. They also produce mannequins and hairstyling tools.

PROFESSIONAL BEAUTY ASSOCIATION

7755 E. Gray Road
Scottsdale, AZ 85260
(480) 281-0424
Website: probeauty.org
Facebook: @professionalbeautyassociation
Instagram: @probeautyassoc
PBA is a trade organization that represents all aspects of the beauty industry.

VOGUE

1 World Trade Center
New York NY 10007
(800) 234-2347
Website: www.vogue.com/magazine
Facebook: @Vogue
Instagram: @voguemagazine

Vogue is generally considered the pinnacle of the fashion magazine industry. Working for them is the ultimate goal of many print stylists.

FOR FURTHER READING

Bolick, Kate. *Becoming a Hairstylist*. New York, NY: Simon & Schuster, 2019.

Daego, Nailah. *Cosmetology State Board Written Practice Exam Book with 5 Mock Exams and 550 Practice Questions*. Independently published, 2023.

Enoch, Joshua. *From Barber to a Business: The Simple Guide to Becoming a Successful Barber*. Independently published, 2021.

Javor, Alexandra. *Hairstyling Kit Checklist: Pack Your Mobile Kit Efficiently for Weddings & Other Events*. Independently published, 2023.

King, Crystal. *Standing Behind the Chair of Your Dreams: A Simple Guide to Cosmetology Career Development*. Independently published, 2019.

Milady. *Milady's Standard Cosmetology* 14th Edition. Clifton Park, NY: Cengage Learning, 2021.

Negron, Raymond. *Hairstylist 101: Tips, Tricks, Tools and Techniques That Turn Beginners into Pros*. Independently Published, 2019.

Torres, Chuka. *The Rich Barber Method: How to Attract Clients, Keep Them, and Charge More*. Independently published, 2020.

INDEX

ABOUT THE AUTHOR

KATHLEEN A. KLATTE is the author of many nonfiction books for children and teens. Topics range from animals and nature to constitutional law to unusual career choices. She lives in New York with one cat and far too many books and Legos.

PHOTO CREDITS

Photo credits:Cover, p. 1 Rawpixel.com/Shutterstock.com; p.3-96 Merydolla// Shutterstock.com; pp. 5, 16 LightField Studios/Shutterstock.com; p. 7 Serhii Bobyk/Shutterstock.com; p.8 https://commons.wikimedia.org/wiki/File:Marie-Antoinette;_koningin_der_Fransen.jpg; p. 10 yamasano708/Shutterstock.com; p. 12 RYO Alexandre/Shutterstock.com; p. 13 khaffizzul hakim/ Shutterstock.com; p. 15 Microgen/Shutterstock.com; p. 18 PeopleImages.com - Yuri A/Shutterstock.com; p. 20 Monkey Business Images/Shutterstock.com; p. 23 BearFotos/Shutterstock.com; p. 25 shisu_ka/Shutterstock.com; p. 27 MarcoGrandi/Shutterstock.com; p. 28 AnnaTamila/Shutterstock.com; p. 30 sebastiancaptures/Shutterstock.com; p. 32 lunamarina/Shutterstock.com; p. 33 Johnstocker Production/Shutterstock.com; p. 34 eyematter/Shutterstock.com; p. 35 Freer/Shutterstock.com; p. 37 Dean Drobot/Shutterstock.com; p. 39 Baloncici/Shutterstock.com; p. 41 hedgehog94/Shutterstock.com; p. 43 Pixel-Shot/Shutterstock.com; p. 45 Prostock-studio/Shutterstock.com; p. 46 New Africa/Shutterstock.com; p. 47 nizas/Shutterstock.com; p. 51 Anirut Thailand/Shutterstock.com; p.53 https://commons.wikimedia.org/wiki/ File:NPG_2008_20_Walker.tif; p. 56 AlexanderZam/Shutterstock.com; p. 57 irishe4kaaa/Shutterstock.com; p. 59 neftali/Shutterstock.com; p. 61 Eric Glenn/Shutterstock.com; p. 62 Parilov/Shutterstock.com; p. 66 Freeograph/ Shutterstock.com; p. 68 Emma'sPhotos/Shutterstock.com; p. 69 imging/ Shutterstock.com; p. 71 Nacho Such/Shutterstock.com; p. 73 Cherkas/ Shutterstock.com; p. 74 Ground Picture/Shutterstock.com; p. 77 Gorodenkoff/ Shutterstock.com; p. 81 Olena Yakobchuk/Shutterstock.com; p. 83 Julian Sarmiento/Shutterstock.com.